For Hattie
from
Carolyn Waitz

Medieval Cats

qui rpus est ualeamus per
uenne. per. de cos mgarta.

Rat eutem marga
reca annonim qum
decim dum ab impio

Medieval Cats

SUSAN HERBERT

A BULFINCH PRESS BOOK
LITTLE, BROWN AND COMPANY
Boston · New York · Toronto · London

FOR MY MOTHER

FRONTISPIECE

St Margaret
French, late 14th century.
(From Backhouse, *Books of Hours*)

Copyright © 1995 by Thames and Hudson Ltd, London

First North American Edition
ISBN 0-8212-2179-5

Library of Congress Catalog Card Number 94-79058

Bulfinch Press is an imprint and trademark of
Little, Brown and Company (Inc.)
Published simultaneously in Canada by
Little, Brown & Company (Canada) Limited

PRINTED IN SINGAPORE

PREFACE

The sensational discovery in 1991 of a cache of delicate paintings beneath a fragmentary pillar of the disused, indeed demolished, Abbey of St Wilderic in the deserted outskirts of the Alsatian village of Tierck-les-Bains set the world of medieval scholarship on its ear. The excavation took place originally because a group of real estate speculators wished to break ground for a giant shopping development, and the labourers who discovered these precious paintings, kept safe in a strange package of straw, took time off from their work to have a good laugh at these funny pictures of cats, of all things — cats in costume, cats as people, cats even as angels!

By the greatest good fortune, a rather well-educated foreman on the site was disturbed by the cackling and guffawing which indicated to him that the workmen were not making the best use of their picks and shovels. With stern demeanour, he relieved them of the paintings and directed them back to their digging. Not until he was home again that evening, preparing to relax in front of the TV set, did he think of the package and unwrap it. Far from laughing at its contents, he felt a prickling of excitement as he examined the paintings. He was reminded of pictures he had seen in his childhood, postcards glimpsed during school visits to museums or churches.

The foreman happened to have a brother who was a priest in a neighbouring parish, and since there seemed to be something of a religious nature about these cat paintings, he took the opportunity of their next meeting to bring them to his brother's attention. Father Alphonse was, understandably, perplexed in the extreme, but was also intelligent enough to take them to a higher ecclesiastical authority, who in turn consulted the head of the Ecole des Beaux-Arts, and before long it was determined by an exceedingly eminent team of experts that these paintings were not only authentic, but a discovery of the first magnitude. What they showed was that some of the greatest masterpieces of miniature painting and illumination had first been sketched out with cats as stand-ins for the characters in the final paintings, and this of course led to a complete reassessment of the role of the cat in medieval life. While the research into this intriguing subject continues, not only in Paris, but also in London, New York and wherever medieval studies are pursued, we felt it was only fair to present a sampling of these long-lost little paintings to the public in the form of this book.

Professor Adolphe Moumoune
University of Châteauroux

St Luke
The Bodmer Hours, Italian, early 15th century
(Pierpont Morgan Library, New York)

St Charlemagne
Les Belles Heures de Jean, duc de Berry,
folio 174, painted by the Limbourg brothers
(The Cloisters, New York).

Entering the Grande Chartreuse
Les Belles Heures de Jean, duc de Berry,
folio 97, painted by the Limbourg brothers
(The Cloisters, New York).

Et eos non sine grandi labore ad locum ubi by
ztelle que uidet inlcopmo steterez duxit et aut. hic
eut locus uester. ibi urgitur ipo epo uuo loo unua
re edificare repit pma domu ordizcartusiensin

King Charles VI Conversing with Pierre Salmon
Pierre Salmon: Questions Asked by Charles VI ...
(Public and University Library, Geneva)

alemon xxantesfois et en plufeurs mautes
par braue experience se fait quons beu et appercen
se grant desir et sa bonne boulente que bous aues
au bien de nous et de nre Poyaume tant par les morales
auttorites exemples et sr feores a nous par hous alleguez

Attending at a Birth
Histoires des Nobles Princes de Hainaut,
painted by Jacques de Guise.

N lan de nre seigne
mil cent quatre hu[tz]
et sept ou mois
d aoust acoucha la royne de fra

January
Les Très Riches Heures de Jean de France, duc de Berry,
painted by the Limbourg brothers.

18

May
Les Très Riches Heures de Jean de France, duc de Berry,
painted by the Limbourg brothers.

August
Les Très Riches Heures de Jean de France, duc de Berry,
painted by the Limbourg brothers.

equiem . pſalmus .
uevere me deus
ſecundum ma
gnam miſeucordiam

tuam
t ſeandum mul
titudmem miſeracio
num tuam dele mi

St Rupert and the Canon Grillinger
The Bible of Peter Grillinger,
Austrian, *c.* 1430.

oncede michi misericors
Deus que tibi placita sut
ardenter conaun stere pau

St Catherine of Alexandria
Hours of William, Lord Hastings.

King René's Book of Love, folio 31.

aduie que autresfoiz lauoit Il beu en lostel du bien damours
Et le salua et luy dist en telle maniere

Icy parle de sa humble Requeste le pour suiuant damours et dit

Oue soiez lee tresbien trouue
Gent pour suiuant bien aprouue
Mon doulx amy humble requeste
Outes moy ou alles en queste

King René's Book of Love, folio 46.

Icy parle lacteur et dit ainsi que?

Quant les trois compaignons earent leues et oyes
Les lettres qui estorent escuptes ou tableau Jlz
furent pensifz trop durement et se regarderent
lun lautre comme tous esbahyz achief de piece le œur qui
plus effort beaulx que nulz des autres seusa et entra
en la maisonnette le premieret ses deux compaignons
entrerent apres mais Jlz trouverent pouure hostel et mal
acoustre Jlz marcherent Jasques aufouer de la maisonnette

King René's Book of Love, folio 51.

Joy parle lacteur et dit amsi que
Ces parolles le cueur Incontinent mist piet aterre
tout couroce et pensongneux de ce que tant lauoit
mue et marcha drost alu mer et entra en la nas
selle et les deux autres compaignons firent Incontinent amse
et habandomerent tous leurs cheuaulx aleure barletz qui
les prirent et les emmerent pour le guerre don de leurs sex

St John on Patmos
Breviary of Queen Isabella of Castile,
painted by a Flemish master.

Scene from Froissart's Chronicle,
French, 15th century.

Cy commence la cinquiesme elyivue
de zenone A paris

Peasants Dancing
Les Heures de Charles d'Angoulême.
(Bibliothèque Nationale, Paris)

King David Playing the Harp
The Hours of Bonaparte Ghislieri

tuelte marie iigadu
omne labia . tu warm

ECCE · ANCILLA ·

Jean de Meun Presenting His Translation to Philip IV of France
Boethius, *De Consolatione Philosophiae,*
painting by Jean Colombe.

A Royal maiefte
Trefnoble prince par
la grace de dieu Roy
de france phelippe
le quart Je Jehan Je mehun qui
Jadie ou romant de la Role puis

St Anne with Patron Saints
The 'Grandes Heures' of Anne of Brittany, Queen of France.
French, 1500/08, painted by Jean Bourdichon.
(Bibliothéque Nationale, Paris)

David and Bathsheba
Hours of the Vasselin Family.

Omine ne i furore
tuo arquas me : ne
qz mña tua corri

Domestic scene from the Da Costa Hours.
Flemish, *c.* 1515.

OVERLEAF:
Job on His Dunghill
Hours of Henry VII,
painted by Jean Bourdichon.